SURRENDER

SURRENDER

Father Walter Ciszek:
Jesuit Priest/Soviet Prisoner

Seamus Dockery

To order additional copies of this book, contact:
Xlibris Corporation
1-888-795-4274
www.Xlibris.com
Orders@Xlibris.com
118505

CONTENTS

PREFACE

SURRENDER is the true story of the vocation of an American Jesuit priest, accused by the Soviet era K.G.B. of being a Vatican spy, who survived fifteen years of hard labor in Siberian prison camps. Father Walter Ciszek not only survived but learned to surrender to God's Providence.

SURRENDER is a narrative digest based entirely on Father Ciszek's two books: *With God in Russia,* (1964), published one year after his release from Russia, and his second book, *He Leadeth Me, (*1973), published nine years later. **SURRENDER** interweaves these two books and telescopes the most dramatic events of Father Ciszek's vocation and steadfast fidelity to that calling through the crucible of unjust imprisonment following the end of World War II.

The profound insights of Father Ciszek's second book illuminate the grim facts of his first book. **SURRENDER** attempts to highlight the evolution of spiritual wisdom in *He Leadeth Me,* embedded in the harsh events depicted in *With God in Russia.* Hopefully, through the relative brevity of **SURRENDER**, the major chords of Father Ciszek's heroic embrace of God's Providence in the most extreme conditions will resonate. The reason why Father Ciszek's cause for Canonization, the process of declaration of Sainthood in the Roman Catholic Church, is currently proceeding should be abundantly evident.

SURRENDER describes not the triumph of human will-power but the freedom of total dependence on God. The paradox of power to love is only born in the powerlessness of surrender of self-will to God's Providence.

With deep respect, I dared to write this narrative digest in the first person voice of Father Walter Ciszek, often using his own words.

Seamus Dockery

GRATITUDES

Gratitude to these Jesuits for their assistance and encouragement: Fr. James Casciotti, Fr. Michael Desjardins, Fr. Daniel Flaherty, Fr. Robert Hamm, Fr. John Henry, Fr. Edward Ifkovits, Fr. James Martin, Fr. J. Allan Panuska, Fr. Thomas Reese, Fr. Peter Schineller, Fr. Raymond Schroth, Fr. William J. Walsh, and Fr. William Watters.

Gratitude to these collaborators for research and resource assistance: Drew Casper, Nick D'Allesandro, John Devecka, Rosie Hanneke, Oleg Manko, John Riina, Richard Sigler, and Russell Sveda.

Gratitude to these benefactors: William Brooke, Fr. Frank Callahan, Fr. David Carey, Frank Fox, Joan and Frank McDermott, Lyde Marie Newman, Carol and James O'Hara, Anita Healy O'Neill, Charles Reeves, Macrina Seitz, and Kathleen and Roger Sullivan.

Gratitude most especially to my generous and exacting editor Nina Carey Tassi and to Mary Jervis at Xlibris for her constant execution of details.

A.M.D.G.

For further information regarding Father Walter Ciszek's Canonization process and prayers, contact: fwccenter@verizon.com.

CHAPTER ONE

BEGINNINGS

I was born stubborn on November 4, 1904 and prided myself on being a bully and known as a street fighter in Shenandoah, PA. Played sports and also played hooky at St. Casimir and had to repeat a year for delinquencies. My father, Martin, ran a saloon and with my mother, Mary, brought a brood of fourteen Polish kids into this coal miner's town. Father once dragged me to the local police station complaining that he couldn't set me straight and maybe they could do better. Didn't scare me but inside I wondered would he abandon me. Shortly after when I blew all my money at an amusement park with the Boy Scouts and arrived home at 1 A.M. he was waiting up worried sick. There were no wallops; he made me breakfast after listening to my story of hitching onto the outside of a train and almost being clipped in a narrow tunnel and killed. He made me breakfast and put me to bed. I knew he loved me and never forgot that breakfast, not even in the Siberian prison many, many years later.

When I was fourteen, out of the blue I decided that I would be a priest. My family thought I was crazed, except my mother who prevailed, and off I went to Sts. Cyril & Methodius Minor Seminary in Orchard Lake, Michigan. The police at the station house had a good laugh.

I scorned the pale-pious sissies in the seminary and snuck at night to the chapel so no one saw me praying. I stayed tough, got up at 4:30 A.M. to run five miles and swim in the lake well into November. During Lent, asking no one's permission, I ate only bread and water for forty days and vowed secretly to go meatless for a year. Nobody dared to squeal on me. I vowed to myself to always do the hardest thing and during summers worked in the fields alone to learn to bear the loneliness while other seminarians went home. Never thought much about how my parents and kin felt about this. Years later in Moscow's dreaded Lubianka prison I would have five years of solitude and my family would believe that I was dead. But back at the seminary, I even dropped playing baseball because I loved it too much. Little did I dream that all this early boot camp self-denial and rigor would prepare me for fifteen years at hard labor in Russian prison camps in Arctic Siberia.

Crisis occured in the seminary when a Jesuit priest gave a retreat and I heard that the Polish Jesuit Saint Stanislas, when in his early teens, walked from Warsaw to Rome to enter the Jesuits back in the 17th Century. That made me think about the Jesuits but I didn't want to join them because that meant putting off Ordination for seven years instead of three in the diocesan priests. But since it was harder to be a Jesuit, I decided that was what I must do. I immediately wrote to the Jesuit General in Rome who happened to fortunately be Polish. I was sure he would understand, and he did. He replied by suggesting I seek out the New York Provincial. Telling no one at the seminary, I hopped a train, this time, inside the train, and with a ticket somehow made my way via the subway up to the Bronx where the Jesuit Provincial had his residence. I arrived unannounced at 7:30 P.M. and this twenty-four year old commenced to shout at the elderly, almost deaf Jesuit who opened the door: "I must be a Jesuit." By ll P.M. they were more or less convinced that I wasn't entirely mad. When I left that residence on Fordham Road I experienced a deep inner consolation: I belonged! Years later that consolation would return, at times, when I celebrated Mass in the dead of winter in the Siberian forests with temperatures of forty degrees below zero.

I waited until the morning I left home in Shenandoah to tell my parents that I was going into the Jesuits. My father shouted "Nothing doing" and I shouted back "No sir, I'm going to St. Andrew." He banged on the table and I banged right back and out the door I went with no blessing or farewell except by mother silently clutching her Rosary beads. My will, not their feelings, was my only concern. Time would change that the hard way in Siberia and I would be the one pressing the beads.

I was twenty-four years old when I entered the Jesuit Novitiate at St. Andrew on Hudson in Poughkeepsie, New York and I was still very rough around the edges. Most of the younger novices were intimidated by my growl and I liked it that way. I was short in stature so I made up for that with swagger and gruffness. I banged pots and pans and hurled wheelbarrels with abandon. They said: "Steer clear of Ciszek; he even races ahead when we say the Rosary in bands of three; he likes to break a sweat when he prays."

Then one fateful day, the Novice Master, Fr. Weber, called me on the carpet and told me flat out that I had to leave. I shot back "I will not leave." He stared me down and growled "Who do you think you are?" That did it; I began to sob, utterly lost. I might lose my heart's desire to be a priest by playing the tough guy. I got a reprieve and slowed my gait and barked less and shortly after, that same Novice Master read a letter from the General of the Jesuits, Father Wlodimir Ledochowski, dated February 24, 1930, seeking courageous priests willing to go into Communist Russia. I sat transfixed. God was speaking to me directly, calling me to this dangerous and daunting mission. I immediately knocked on the Master's door and told him, with absolute conviction, that this was God's mission for me: Russia was my destiny. I was completely sure of myself and had no doubts. Impulsive? Yes. Remember how Saul got knocked to the ground before he became St. Paul? Sometimes God does speak in thunderbolts.

After taking Vows as a Jesuit on September 8, 1930 I wrote again to the General of the Jesuits in Rome asking to be sent to Russia. This time I had permission to do so. Fr. General accepted my request but first there were more years of study: theology in Rome at the Gregorian and the Russicum where I could study the Russian language, literature and history, as well as the Oriental Liturgy. The calling and impulsive "yes" were being shaped by study and prayer and learning to wait. The tough guy was being disciplined by the slow and thorough training of the missionary. From the start, Ignatius, the founder of the Jesuits, educated his own first before he sent them to the ends of the earth. I came to love Russia and her people during my twenty-three years there, even though I was their prisoner, falsely accused and sentenced. At the Russicum in Rome I had to learn the Oriental Liturgy; I couldn't stand the lengthly and repetitious Oriental Rite, but that, of course, made me more determined to immerse myself. Born stubborn!

I was ordained a Jesuit priest on June 23, 1937 and offered my first Mass at the Basilica of St. Paul, that zealot tough apostle to the Gentiles who trekked and sailed all over the known world enduring hardships, chains, and imprisonment. Little did I guess how closely I would follow in his footsteps. While at the Russicum I became fast friends with Nestrov, a native Russian, a big bear with a bass voice and Maker, a Pole mischief maker who made us laugh. We named ourselves The Three Musketeers. My dreams were just beginning to be fulfilled but shortly thereafter Fr. General summoned us to tell us that entering Russia was then impossible but that he could send us on a mission into Poland to minister as priests in Albertin. This was a great emotional let-down but I never doubted that one day I would be sent into Russia and so, with the General's blessing my race to the finish line was begun and my ministry as a priest began.

CHAPTER TWO

MISSION IN POLAND: ALBERTIN

My mission in Poland began teaching Ethics to young Jesuits at a seminary and catechism to children. On weekends I was a "horse and buggy priest" saying Mass at countryside parishes near Slonim. By November 1938 we received warnings from the American Embassy to leave Poland. I insisted on staying where we were needed. By Sept. 1, 1939 Hitler invaded Poland and Russians were on the Eastern border. When the Russians invaded Albertin I was the only priest there. They ransacked all the books in the library, toppled the Sacred Heart statue, and from the back pews of the chapel mocked me as I celebrated Mass. By the time I got to giving the sermon those thugs were my target and I bellowed my disgust at their shameless heckling and that shut them up, for the time being. The next morning when I returned to the chapel, the tabernacle door was wide open and the Blessed Sacrament gone. My heart sank; this was their revenge for being humiliated. My little victory of anger at them had consequences. My street tough skills had lessons to learn.

Another telegram arrived from the American Embassy in Moscow warning us to leave but I would not run away and abandon my flock. Stand your ground. Suddenly Fathers Nestrov and Maker returned and we Three Musketeers went to the Bishop for advice and he directed us to close the Oriental Mission and even suggested we slip into Russia to serve those most in need, if our Jesuit Superiors approved. We were immediately excited by this daring challenge and as we left that meeting we all agreed that "We'll be in Russia in the Spring." Workers were needed in the Ural Mountain factories. Our Jesuit Superior agreed on this bold mission and we then visited the Archbishop in Lvov for his permission. He agreed and commissioned us to study the situation in Russia for one year to see if it was possible to do priestly work there. He was as bold as St. Paul heading into Asia and heathen lands two thousand years ago. We were Jesuits and Jesuits were shock-troop missionaries. That invitation of Father General that I had heard in my novitiate days was sounding loud and clear in my heart: *Adsum*: I am ready.

With the assistance of wily Fr. Makar, my Polish accomplice, we got Polish I.D. papers.

My cover name was Wladimir Lypinski and Fr. Nestrov was Kuralski. In no time time we were hired by a lumber company. We returned to the Archbishop for his blessing on our covert mission into Russia. We looked on puzzled when the Archbishop tore a half page from his prayer book and handed it to us. He instructed us that if we sent him a message it must come with our half of the page as proof it was from us. He knew the game we were just beginning to understand. His Sisters gave us a huge loaf of bread for the train trip ahead and we knelt for his blessing. We departed, packed our Mass kit, and made our Confessions.

On March 15, 1940 we boarded Boxcar 89725 at the Lvov Train Station; twenty-five to a boxcar, mostly Warsaw Jews and their families, fleeing the Nazis and dreaming of escaping to Communist paradise. A dream too soon shattered upon arrival at the work camps. The Sisters' loaf of bread and our fatback rations were shared and soon depleted on this 1,500 mile train ride with frequent stops and daylong delays. When I begged a peasant farm woman at a train stop for water with a Jewish boy at my side, she cursed us and I cursed her back with slang from the streets of Shenandoah I hadn't uttered for years. Fortunately, the Jewish youth didn't understand Pennsyvania *dutch* and didn't know that I was a priest. We told no one that we were priests. As the train moved on, to the clicking of the wheels, I kept repeating in my head: I am ready, I am ready, I am ready Lord. Nestrov nudged me as he spotted a border sign: we had just crossed into Russia. It was on the Feast of St Joseph, March 19. We were exhilarated but as we looked at the vast barren stretches of land, loneliness settled in. All we knew was left behind. Slowly it dawned on me that I might never return. It would be twenty-three years later that I did return to America, long after I had given up all hope of ever returning.

We arrived two weeks later in Chusovoy, 750 miles northeast of Moscow and soon walked in pouring rain to the lumber yard in Teplaya-Gora. The work camp barracks were not home sweet home, but the workers' families gave them a semblance of humanity. The work was hauling logs from the river's freezing water and your hands bled and bled until they hardened with callouses. That was the summer of 1940 and I was thirty-six years old and had to shape up fast to earn my daily bread. Thank God I had done all that running and swimming in November cold water back in the seminary days. God knew then where He would send me. I had always wanted the harder way and now I was getting my fill.

In secret, on the rare work break, Fr. Nestrov and I celebrated Mass on a tree stump altar in a secluded part of the forest surrounded by stillness. Not far off were multitudes of Communist atheists and a few old-timers who still occasionally muttered "Gospodi." Holy Mother Russia was in a deep sleep, almost a coma. But we had memorized the Mass and prayed in that forest and I knew deep joy, believing that God was incarnate here in this wilderness of disbelief. We were here and so was God.

However, after we finished Mass and returned to the barracks our dreams of tending God's flock seemed useless. How easy it was to slip into brooding in this wasteland. I resolved that work itself had to be our prayer, our mission. Hauling lumber wasn't so far from the labor that the son of Joseph the carpenter had done two thousand years ago. Jesus had callouses too, and that and the sweat of my brow shook the brooding away.

Other jobs came my way: being a truck driver seemed like a break from hauling logs until I was stranded at 2 A.M. on a dirt road in forty degree below zero temperatures trying to fix a fuel line with frozen fingers. At dawn another trucker saved me from freezing to death. My cheeks were frozen blue and took months to heal.

As the winter finally passed, there were some occasions when picking blueberries we could strike up a conversation, especially with the teenagers, who were interested in religion. God for them was an exotic and forbidden topic endlessly ridiculed by Communist propaganda all around them. But our mission as priests seemed hopeless and futile. That God wanted us there didn't make much sense. I had told only a few others in the hospital when I was convalescing that I was a priest.

Suddenly I was sent back to the lumber brigade. A few mornings later I was shaken awake at 3AM by strangers: the NKVD, the Secret Police. They arrested me and Nestrov as German spies. They shoved our Mass Kit in our faces demanding to know our secret plans of sabotage. Little did we know that this Ural Mountain area also had munition factories. Off we were hauled to the Chusovoy jail almost laughing that they believed we priests were German spies and that our Mass Kit was thought a secret weapon loaded with nitro and codes. We didn't laugh for long.

CHAPTER THREE

RUSSIAN IMPRISONMENT: LUBIANKA

The pressure was on the outpost jailers at Chusovoy to get Nestrov and myself to confess. When we could only admit that we were on a priestly mission, they took that as a ruse to hide our dirty secrets. Didn't take long before they were spitting curses in our faces and pummeling our heads with their fists. They left us on the cell floor, utterly disgusted with us and utterly empty-handed.

After two weeks we were then dumped in a truck and loaded on a train, not knowing what had prompted this or where we were headed in the night. Bruises I knew from Shenandoah street brawls, but these black and blue welts made no sense. During that endless train ride in the darkness, Christ's battered face and thorn-crowned head stared me in the face: terminus unknown.

Finally we arrived at the big-house and the ritual of admittance began: we were stripped naked, deloused with water hoses and then prodded and poked by stern faced women doctors. Waiting in lines, this went on and on all night. Without sleep for forty-eight hours we finally were shoved into solitary cells. At 7 A.M. alarm bells burst your eardrums and guards shouted "Podium": get up. The steel bolts snapped open and a food pail was deposited. My first food in the last thirty-six hours. I did mean "Thank You Lord" as I licked the pail clean. There was no chair and only a slop bucket in the corner of the cell. The only window was covered with tin sheeting except for a sliver of light at the very top where there was a vent for air. One light bulb was on-always on, day and night. Guards announced that once you were up on your feet in the in the morning off your mat until sleep at 10 P.M. You could not sit at all on the bed and the bolt slit on the door could bang open day and night so that the guards could monitor your every move. All privacy was gone and the stillness of total isolation descended. The guards even wore felt covering on their shoes so that you could never hear them coming or going. Entombment was absolute. Even trips to the bathroom were monitored.

As this isolation descended on me and the fetus of depression was borne within, I soon countered with a Daily Order to cope: Morning Offering prayer, Angelus when I heard church bells outside the prison walls, then three Rosaries in Latin, Polish, and Russian, noontime Examen of Conscience, resentments and self-pity had to be exorcized daily. Then I recited the entire Mass from memory each day, then hymns and poems and Scripture passages I could recall from years of study and prayer. Then a work-out of physical routines, repeated often at intervals, which helped to keep longings for food distracted momentarily. I also took to polishing the hard wood floors over and over to erase hunger pangs.

This Daily Order was rudely interrupted day and night by the doorbolt suddenly slammed open when I was hustled down long corridors to the subterranean interrogation cells. These interrogators were not the brute jailhouse cops of Chusnovoy, but professional inquisitors who hammered you over and over with the same questions to find the slightest crack of inconsistency and deviation. I was stunned to find out how much they already knew about me: my true name, the date and place of my birth in the USA, that I was a Jesuit priest from Albertin and had studied in Rome.

They charged me with Section 58:10:02 of their Criminal Code: subversive activity. The NKGB interrogator brushed aside my denials with repeated mocking commands to tell the truth like a good priest should. These sessions usually lasted four and five hours, most begun in the middle of the night and ending in the wee hours of the dawn. Despite this rigor, I felt that I could take them on and soon reduced my replies to blunt "yes" and "no" with as little elaboration as possible. They had to know that I was no patsy in their hands. Ciszek was a tough guy.

Even after these exhausting sessions, the wake-up clang was always at 7 A.M. and so my days began wondering how did they know so much and where was I and why was I here. How did they know so much? I would later understand their network of spies was everywhere! But above all, how was this God's plan for me? Where was my priestly ministry in this? I did not then understand God's Providence in the here and now.

Soon after the interrogations began, so too did the sirens wail at all hours and bombs rocked the prison walls. We were hustled out of our cells into underground shelters. When the bombing struck a direct hit, all the prisoners were marched to the central train station, surrounded by fierce guard dogs, and crammed into boxcars where we sat for days with no food and water. In those close quarters I found out that our prison was LUBIANKA, the dreaded warehouse prison of the NKGB in Moscow, and that those were German bombing runs blasting us relentlessly. There were twenty prisoners crammed into 10'x10' train compartments. We got our first food in days: wonderful rye bread baked by peasants at Atkarsh. We then rolled on for thirteen days until we reached a temporary prison, a school complex in Saratov away from the bombs. We showered in the school house with one hundred and fifty of us squeezed into prison school rooms meant for fifty. Finally some company! My companions were all political prisoners, many professionals of all sorts, and many professors and teachers. We even began giving lectures on our specialties to occupy ourselves in such close quarters, amused that we were held captive in a schoolhouse. The grimness of our situation was apparent one morning when the bloody corpse of a "spy" from our own company was discovered in the shower stall.

The interrogations continued and now attempts were made to turn me into a counter-spy if I would cooperate. Not this Polish/American Jesuit priest!

In the middle of the night I was interrogated by a new, almost boyish interrogator who was so inept I almost laughed in his face. When he banged on the table to scare me, I had to force myself not to laugh and remembered how I had banged the table back at my father's house when I departed to join the Jesuits. But I did smile inside: I could tough this out. This boyish interrogator even attempted to ply me with tea and sandwiches and I stared him down and refused his good-cop ruse. Refusing any offer of food was not easy and later that night I gnawed on a ham bone found in a waste bucket. But I had refused their tea and cookies and stood tall.

It was not long before we trained back to Lubianka and now the interrogations got even more intense. At my next session, begun at 9 P.M. and ending at 4 A.M., I encountered NKGB "Professor" Sedov, a thirty-five year old seasoned and formidable expert interrogator whom I would duel with every day and night for the coming months. Over and over the same questions: Why did I go as a worker to the Urals? My spiritual mission explanation was summarily dismissed with scorn and Sedov was absolutely convinced I was hiding valuable secrets. In fact, his stubbornness reminded ✓ me of my own. I had met my match!

The usual one month of interrogation was extended to two months: Sedov was not accustomed to such prisoner resistance and it became clear that he intended to break me. He would not have his success record defiled by an arrogant Jesuit priest. He then produced as his trump card the torn half page from the prayer book the Archbishop had given us, which was hidden in our confiscated Mass kit. He expected me to squirm when he slapped the crumpled torn page on the desk. He accused me of collaboration with the Germans but then he got an even better idea: I must be a Vatican spy. That caught his imagination and he almost salivated at the idea. What a coup for him. His first Vatican spy. He pressed harder and harder until finally after endless rounds of my "yes" and "no" he screamed "Out!" Even the guards looked down at the floor to avoid seeing their cool boss lose it.

Shortly thereafter a Polish officer prisoner was put in my cell, and I admitted to him that I was a priest when he told me that he was a Roman Catholic with a family and that he would be released if he could get some explanation of my covert spy mission. I could only give him the same truth I had already given Sedov.

On a Sunday morning, 2 A.M., I was given food and hot tea and I believed that finally they believed my story. I ate and drank the tea which was so bitter I asked for sugar and they even gave me that to my surprise. I suddenly felt dizzy and soon fell into a blackout, losing all consciousness. When I finally awoke I felt like I had fallen down ten flights of stairs. There was a pen in my hand, and the guards standing over me were laughing. I looked up and the walls of the room were blazing red and caving in on me and I could not speak at all. They then forced me to take some pills, and then I was dragged back to my own cell. That session had lasted forty-eight hours. God knows what I had signed. I didn't. From then on I trusted no one but God. I almost hated Sedov.

A week later I was moved to a detention cell. I was informed that as I had confessed; I was now charged with espionage, not just subversion. The charge was #58:6 and the sentence: fifteen years of hard labor in Siberia. The signed document in front of me was dated July 26, 1942. I sat stunned. The guards couldn't stop laughing at my stupified blank stare of disbelief.

But I didn't cry on the outside. Inside, I was broken: that was my signature on the confession.

"Gradually my prayer shifted from what I wanted to happen to what God wanted: Thy will be done."

Chapter Four

LUBIANKA 'CONFESSION' REVISITED

I wrote the first version of my "confession" at Lubianka one year after I left Russia. The following details more accurately the collapse of my will power. This second version was written in my second book, published nine years after my liberation from Siberia.

As I had written, when the interrogations began I was initially untroubled and stood tall in my self-confidence. Once again, recall that I was born stubborn and grew up strong-willed and had cultivated that will power with ascetic/macho discipline in the early seminary and later in the Jesuits. As the months of interrogation, night and day, continued, self-doubt and fear of collapse began seeping into my soul. I did pray more and more, but fear and doubt did not disappear. I prayed for more food, but more food never came. I prayed for the conversion of my interrogators, but none ever happened. Gradually my prayer shifted from what I wanted to happen to what God wanted: Thy will be done. I was entering the same garden of agony where he had sweat blood. Lubianka was becoming a school of prayer. Letting God be God was gradually finding foot in my soul: to rely on God I had to let go.

The interrogators wrote down every answer and asked the same questions over and over and then read back to me what they had written; it was like an echo chamber always filtered through their distortions. In time I simply gave up arguing. Resentment and repugnance deepened in the bowels of my soul. It became impossible to spar another round. I put my head down and dropped my guard.

I finally told them: I'll tell the truth and cooperate. I wasn't going to fight their interpretation of the facts I had admitted. What a mistake! I tried to change my tactic and reverse my course but there was no going back and they smelled the fear and pressed on and on. This nightmare was endless and I wanted it to be over. It was a living death by a thousand bloodless nicks. I was caving in. I prayed and prayed, asking the Holy Spirit to rescue me. I delayed signing the "confession" but I felt abandoned by God. I wanted to say "I won't sign" but those words never came. I was angry at myself, my weakness. I was very afraid. Sedov, the interrogator, could sense my swaying in the wind and asked, "What's wrong Vladimir Martinovich?" (my imposter name). I responded "I can't sign this the way it's written. It's not what I said or did. You know I'm not the spy you describe so cleverly and completely in this report."

Enraged, Sedov shouted to the guards, "Get rid of him. You stupid priest, you will be dead before sunset." They moved toward me. I was paralyzed. Stunned into submission. I picked up the pen and began signing each of the hundred-page plus document of "confession."

It was finally over. It was done. I was done. My will had collapsed completely.

Back in my cell I shook uncontrollably like a fish flapping for air, dying out of its element. The reproaches welled up, first at myself and then at God Himself. Why hadn't He simply struck me dead with a heart attack before this disgrace? I was so ashamed of this Walter Ciszek. I had shamed my Church, my priesthood, the Jesuits, my own father and mother, brothers and sisters.

Slowly, days later I began to lift my head up out of the guilt pit with tentative gestures.

Wasn't I nearly out of mind when I signed? Wasn't the signing an animal-like urge for survival?

Was this a free and deliberate choice? The Jesuit training in moral theology began its rescue mission. Finally, distinctions gave way and the root of my shame was exposed by a single word: "I."

I had believed in my own ability to counter evil, to slay the dragon. I had almost relied completely on myself, just as I did in street fights in Shenandoah. Here in Lubianka I was flattened by my own hand signing page after page as the guards laughed and Sedov smiled, ever so slightly. The words from the Book of Wisdom came to mind: "Like gold in the fire he tried them." Then the terrible truth spoke up: the stronger the ingredient of self develops in our lives, the more severe must our humiliations be in order to purify us.

I crouched in my cell and shook, but this shaking brought me to my senses. This moment of failure was in itself a great grace. It was not Sedov, not the NKVD versus Walter Ciszek. It was God versus Walter Ciszek. The Novice Master had asked me long ago when I challenged his order to leave the novitiate: "Who do you think you are?" I thought that nobody could call the shots but Walter Ciszek. Now I let myself cry openly. This time I knelt down and surrendered to God. Like Peter at the gate of the courtyard Gethsemane I had failed God. I could not save myself from myself.

I now had been given the greatest grace: a trial that I could not bear with my own powers. God could and would save me so that I could endure to the finish, whatever time and place that was to be in His Providence.

I would never again try to stand alone. His Providence embraced my shattered self and I began to breathe again. Now I knew in the marrow of my bones: never go it alone.

CHAPTER FIVE

FOUR MORE YEARS
IN LUBIANKA (1942-46)

Now that I had signed a "confession" and been sentenced to fifteen years at hard labor in Siberia I expected to leave Lubianka but for the next four years I remained in Lubianka, with slight detours, as a detainee. There were no more interrogations for one year and two months. Soon after I recovered from my humiliation at confessing, a female guard informed me that Lubianka had a library and that I could request books. I was still in solitary and I became a hermit with no interrogations to distract me from my rituals of prayer and meditation. I almost forgot how to speak but devoured books, reading almost a book a day, reading from after lunch until supper and then until lights out. They never did turn off the night lights. Despite reading Lenin, Marx, and Tolstoy and Russian history filled with distortions about the Church, I still polished the oak floors to keep my mind off food. But even as I prayed I was still terrified that I might fail completely and even lose my faith in God. The struggle to let go of self-reliance didn't happen once and for all, not yet.

After a year and two months the interrogations re-commenced for supplementary information and continued at irregular intervals for the next three years. They prodded. Did I recall any scandals while at the Russicum in Rome? They also made me propositions. Be a chaplain in England (Russia was now an ally with the British and U.S.A.) or a Russian Orthodox post if I would denounce the "Fascist" Pope Pius XII? Or better yet why not marry a young bride, courtesy of KGB? What did I know about the 100,000 Poles reported to have died in the Russian onslaughts? That atrocity was being investigated by an English Commission with a Polish Bishop on the Commission. I thought to myself: Did the KGB think angels flew into my cell undetected by their radar? Had they read about St. Paul's angelic warnings when he was imprisoned? I was somewhat amused and flattered.

Sedov, my tormentor from the past, re-entered the scene to coordinate a personal interview with Beria, the Head of KGB. The interview was cancelled when Beria had more important matters, but that told me they were still convinced I knew more than I had admitted to in my "confession." Their Vatican spy myth captivated them. They wanted me to sign another document that further blackened the Fascist Pope and the Vatican. Propaganda was a valuable tool. Sedov snickered when I played dumb, as he called it, and shook his head with the comment: "I don't know how you are still alive."

I knew how: it was God's Providence and not my fortitude that kept me from falling into that whirlpool of despair.

Suddenly I was transferred in 1944 to Butirka, another prison in Moscow. Another tactical maneuver to break me. I found myself in a damp, unheated, and putrid smelling 30'x30' cell crowded with one hundred and twenty inmates. So, from hermit's cell with book privileges to stuffed cages. Gradually, despite the stench, I came to enjoy the company in that unruly mob of spoon banging inmates who even managed to scrounge shreds to smoke and invent fire with furious rubbing of wooden spoons.

How did I survive this rough mob? I sought out fellow Poles, but even more importantly I listened to their stories and came to understand and sympathize with their hardships. Self-pity gets pushed aside when others expose their scars and grieving over parents, wives, and children abandoned, robbed, and raped. Sorrows like these either turn you to cursing the universe or caring for the wounded. I listened and prayed over their wounds. I often couldn't sleep at night, not only because of the stench, but more so because of the screams from the nightmares of those who did sleep. As I lay awake, trying to pray, I often heard that rasping intake of air that was the rattle of death. Only with death were they then at rest. I prayed for their speedy flight to peace everlasting.

Then, on January 25, who enters our pen but my old Musketeer friend from the Russicum and Albertin days in Poland, Father Nestrov, the Russian Bear. We embraced, laughing, swearing, and crying. What a gift, even though I knew the KGB knew all about the clever gifts of the Greeks at Troy. The arrival of Nestrov was no accident. We heard each other's confessions and later even improvised skits just to laugh again. I played Stalin to his slow-witted true believer comrade pestering Stalin about his seaside *dachas*, fancy cars, caviar and vodka. Comrade kept asking "Where's mine?" The listening inmates around us would start chanting "Where's mine comrade, where's mine?" A few guards even laughed before they shut us up.

During these seven months in Butirka I did actually write to Stalin, not to plead my release but to petition that my relatives and religious superiors be told that I was alive. Much later, after I was liberated, I found out that the Jesuits had assumed that I was dead and had requested fellow Jesuits to offer the customary Masses for the repose of my soul. But God figured out how to save me, both soul and body.

Suddenly, after seven months in the pits of Butirka, I was transferred again and said "*Gospodi*" to Nestrov. I never saw him again.

Back in Lubianka, but now no private cell. Eight in a cell this time where we even played chess with a brilliant, comic chess expert named Nikita, who took on all seven of us at once. He caught us cheating and still won, as always.

Lubianka was a hard school, but a good one. My major lesson: <u>Faith and prayer do not change reality, but they do give it meaning.</u>

Suddenly one night we heard cheering from outside the walls of Lubianka and could also hear the booming of fireworks. Even the guards were cheering outside our cells. The war was over, the Germans had surrendered.

Still, there were more interrogations but at the final one I was told, "This is your last chance." When I refused to sign a document detailing my willingness to become a counter-spy stationed in Rome, Sedov said dryly, "Take him away." I thought that meant either a firing squad then and there or Siberia.

How I was resigned and ready for either fate follows.

CHAPTER SIX

MY CONVERSION IN LUBIANKA

Eight years after my final liberation from Russia, I revisited how I finally had the courage to refuse signing an agreement to be a Soviet counter-spy for the KGB.

Near the end of the four years in Lubianka and Butirka, as the interrogations and propositions continued, I reached a point of despair and lost hope. I was given a choice: cooperate or be executed. I had been at this juncture before when I had signed my "confession." I was powerless to cope with it anymore. A fit of blackness I had never known before enshrouded me. In that deadlock grip I was afraid of myself and even lost the last shreds of faith in God. In that dark night I lost sight of God. In fear and trembling I cried out. I was going under and only He could rescue me from drowning. Thoughts of suicide flickered in my mind.

Suddenly I was consoled and the turmoil calmed as I remembered Christ's agony in the garden of Gethsemane. His words of total self-surrender, "Thy will, not mine, be done," steadied my soul. I watched him soaked in that bloody sweat as he was stripped of his fears and doubts whether he could undergo his crucifixion. He surrendered and as all self-reliance drained from him he was lifted up, embraced by his Father.

Now the way was clear. Follow him. Join him. Alone, I too was powerless but as I let go of my will and fears and surrendered, at that moment, I was set free. I saw clearly what I must do: abandon myself totally to God's Providence and I did it.

I crossed over, letting go of all control of my life ahead. That one decision has affected every subsequent moment of my life.

A wave of confidence and happiness warmed my entire body. I had been to the tomb of death and now I was resurrected in Christ. I was still in prison but not imprisoned by myself. I felt relieved of all responsibility for future outcomes. He leadeth me. I no longer dreaded the next interrogation.

I told Sedov that I was willing to do whatever they proposed. I was perfectly relaxed and detached and Sedov knew I had changed but didn't know why. When the document of agreement to be a KGB counter-spy was put before me, I looked him in the eye, smiled, and simply refused to sign.

By surrendering to God, I had finally won the freedom to say no. At that moment the firing squad had become not executioners but ministers of grace if that was what God choose for me.

God choose Siberia for me and so did the KGB. So be it.

CHAPTER SEVEN

HARD LABOR IN SIBERIA

I had been arrested in Poland in 1941 and left Lubianka in 1946 with the same clothes on my back but my shoes stayed behind, left in the repair shop. We boarded the train in Moscow in the heat of June. There were many women prisoners with babies on board and we were crammed, twenty to a compartment, by the guards with their dogs barking at our heels. No sooner were we settled in and moving than the thug/thieves prisoners begin to rob us of whatever food or clothing they wanted. The guards ignored them. I held tight to the slip-on cloth sandals another prisoner had given me and with the thieves' curses ringing in my ears I fell asleep trying to pray.

We finally reached Vologda, the transport prison where we were sorted by nationality for work brigades. The days of sitting in a cell reading books were no more. Most of the men stripped to their trousers with the heat, and one former army officer who was a political prisoner challenged us to stand up to the thugs but no one dared budge. No other priest except myself was in this brigade. I swapped my only prized possession, a leather valise from seminary days that had survived Lubianka, for a loaf of bread which I shared with my small band of fellow Poles.

By this time I had sores on my body from the parasites feeding on me. Food riots broke out but when we were stripped naked and washed down we calmed down while our clothes were disinfected. A meat-rack selection followed and as a so-called Vatican spy I was assigned to a brigade destined for the far north within the Arctic Circle for the hardest labor. Even when I told a Polish doctor that I was a priest, nothing interfered with that sentence. The thieves were like parasites, survivors. My question was: would I survive?

We then boarded a tug-boat barge on the Yenisay River headed north to Dudinka by the end of July. Didn't take long with the stench and engine vibrations below deck to incite riots between the political prisoners and the thief/thugs. The guards didn't hesitate to sweep just over our heads with machine gun fire. With just a few shot dead we were stunned into calming down. The dead were tossed overboard.

At Camp Krasnoyarsk, our barracks were circled with barbed wire and a no-man zone. Cross that line and you were shot. Our labor was shoveling mountains of coal onto conveyor belts to load the barges. I was in the bowels of the barge shoveling the coal off the conveyor belt; either you kept up or you got buried. At the depot I finally met another priest, a Fr. Casper, who I would later learn actually celebrated Mass there in the camp, in secret, despite fellow-prisoner spies.

A huge canvas tent with the ground for a floor was our barrack where we slept in our work clothes, head to heel: Chinese, Germans, Poles, and Russians. At 6 A.M. an iron pipe gong startled us awake and the morning meal was our only food until 6 P.M. You shoveled all day ducking flying lumps of coal from the conveyor belt, some chunks the size of your head. Keep shoveling and ducking or you were easily buried alive. As I emerged from the barge I was black as the coal, aching all over. My daily exercises in Lubianka helped to condition me but were too effete for this grueling marathon but I survived. *overly refined*

We were strip-searched at the gate before returning to our tent/barrack. A hidden coal-chunk could be a weapon, I suppose. After gulping down supper I headed for my crawl space and slept until the iron gong sounded for another agonizing round of hard labor. Now I knew what those words meant. Every muscle was so tight I couldn't move in the morning to get out of bed, but I did, day after day.

When I finally settled into the daily grind, after supper and late into the night I met with Fr. Casper and celebrated Mass for the first time in five years. Here at last I felt joy again and despite the danger we celebrated Holy Mass often and even heard confessions there in a safe pocket surrounded by those few we came to trust. I could finally minister as a priest again.

Food for the exhausted body was a constant obsession and when I forced down a sour smelling bean soup the only relief was a three-day rest from work due to severe diarrhea. I'll spare you the details of the boils all over my back and legs. When the temperature sank to thirty degrees below in October we were moved from the tent to wooden barracks that were clean and warm.

At the terminal an American ship docked and I desperately wanted to send a message to my sisters and Religious Superiors when I was brought on board to translate some inventory documents but I was constantly guarded. I lost my chance. I left the American ship broken-hearted as it set sail for my long-lost homeland.

As the thirty degrees dipped to forty degrees below zero, a fear that I would never see spring again gripped me. A kind doctor in the camp coached me into a brief hospital reprieve. My recuperation was rewarded with a new work detail: twelve-hour stints in the frozen river dynamiting lumber loose for loading onto barges. This opus lasted until the River froze solid in late November. I never was a slacker and committing to the work, body and soul, renewed my strength. Only a strapping twenty-year old Russian farmer boy outdid my quota. This was the work God gave me this day. This work was now my prayer. So be it.

Some of us were then moved even further north to Norilsk which was deep into the Arctic Circle where we were on construction crews dragging barrels like work horses until the May thaw. When the thaw came, our recreation was louse hunting and finally the luxury of a warm bath that I will never forget. Feeling better, I got into a brawl with some thief/thugs over scraps of bread. They beat me badly and dumped me outside in a snow bank where I was found just soon enough and brought to the infirmary for mending. This old street-tough guy had met his match.

I survived that beating and was moved to another camp and became a number: Zero-One-One-One for food call and work detail. They erased your identity with that number. I was on another construction crew building, an ore processing plant, and it was there that I made friends with Mikhail who was to become the leader of a prisoner rebellion.

The thief/thug prisoners never did their work quota and were ingenious at work slow-downs. Even most of the political prisoners were fed up with ten hour straight construction crews building apartment houses in Norilsk in forty degree below temperatures in the dead of winter.

But life was better in the Camp during off-work hours and there was even camaraderie among your own band of brothers. Fr. Victor had an office assignment and there we continued to celebrate Mass for the believers and hear confessions but we were watched and were repeatedly warned not to do any religious work. Informers, for extra bread and less work, were always around waiting.

The next move to Camp #4 was a huge enterprise bossed by a General Zveriev who knew how to make that big Copper Factory produce over its quota. This Camp was almost a clubhouse with card playing, holidays, and even movies, provided you broke your back working to exceed quotas and deadlines. There were nine priests here; all said Mass regularly. There was even central heating but at 5A.M. close to four thousand prisoners were then pushed to the limit until 7 P.M. Exhausted, we returned to gulp down a hearty soup nicknamed '*Mirovaya*' (marvelous) because it was so thick with potatoes, vegetables, and even scraps of meat, sometimes.

This regimen of exhausting work followed by reprieves and better food and even holidays induced more depression among the inmates. Tasting some pleasure, they recalled how sweet life could be, had been. Some prisoners who had increased their credit by exceeding quotas could even afford a woman for twenty-five rubles. Yes, there were women prisoners in another section and guards could be bribed. Some of the younger men even resorted to other men for sexual release.

Shortly after, I came down with a high fever and was taken to the camp hospital for four whole days of rest. There I met another Polish doctor whom I told that I was a priest. He arranged for me to become a medical orderly and for three months I worked in the pharmacy, an easy job. It was there in that sanctuary that Fr. Victor, Fr. Joe, Fr. Casper, and three Orthodox priests celebrated Mass every night surrounded by doctors and aides. God would not be shut out even in the vast wilderness of the Siberian Arctic Circle. I was with God in Russia. God was incarnate here, with me, through me, in me.

When it was discovered that my medical records were doctored to keep me on light duty in the pharmacy, I was sent outside again to work on another crew as an electrician, about which I knew nothing. One of my pal inmates, Aloysha, cracked up laughing when I crossed two live wires and was jolted with 320 volts. I was knocked out for half an hour and then demoted to under electrician only to subsequently step on another live hot high voltage cable that melted the soles of my work boots. Aloysha laughed again proclaiming *Miraculo* in an Italian accent. Maybe it was a miracle? Again I was reassigned.

Next to our Camp #4 was Camp #5 where Fr. Victor helped ease the burdens of many women prisoners through pregnancies and child caring. There were also Ukrainian nun prisoners who supplied the priests with bread and wine for Mass which were smuggled from the villages that supplied the work camps. During these exchanges we heard confessions, sometimes written on scraps of paper where conversation was impossible and we gave furtive signs of absolution walking near their barricade. So, my ministry as a priest continued in Siberia.

News leaked into the camps that Stalin was nearing death in January of 1953 and this created more unrest in the camps. Prison beatings for infractions and work slowdowns increased and the guards increased lock-ups and strip searches at all hours during the nights. Prison informers, when exposed, were stabbed to death in the showers and brigade foremen who pushed fellow prisoners too hard were dumped into cement foundation pools.

In March of 1953 Stalin himself was dead and even here in Siberia that news was a seismic shock that created a power vacuum. Revolt had been fermenting in the camps and Mikhail emerged as a leader instigating work slowdowns. When five workers had trespassed into the forbidden zone between camps the tower guards riddled them down with machine guns: two killed and three wounded. The camp was in an uproar of protest and Mikhail commanded that we strike and take control of the factory where we were working.

Officials arrived and allowed us to conduct a funeral for the prisoners executed and there was a truce and we returned to work. But suddenly the leaders of the strike were carted off and troops surrounded the Camp and seized control of all who had been on 'strike.' I was caught up in the dragnet, whacked in the head and marched to a huge empty pit where soldiers with machine guns lined us up at the edge of the grave. It was clear that we were going to be executed. I hurriedly made an Act of Contrition as thoughts of my family and my Jesuit brothers raced in my mind. I closed my eyes and froze, waiting to hear the order "Fire." Instead we heard a motor car approach and the General himself shouted "Halt." Only the ringleaders were shot and the rest of us were warned that there would be no pardon the next time. The General needed workers and knew more was accomplished by his pardon than dozens more dead workers.

News from Moscow arrived in the camps that with Stalin's death, changes for the better for all would soon occur. We priests were even allowed to celebrate Mass openly and large crowds attended. But with the Spring thaw and further easement in the camps, many prisoners broke down. Once that tight grip was relaxed, the prisoners felt the pain of this inhuman situation. A strange gloom settled over this hopeless internment and the silence at night was sometimes broken by hysterical laughs, and suicides increased. We prayed over the dead before they were bundled out.

Quotas were not being met and suddenly at 1 A.M. searchlights swept the camps and machine gun fire erupted. The easement had failed to produce results and this ambush announced a return to strict discipline and enforcement. Water hoses were turned on the women prisoners and a posse of known leaders were carted off to squat outside on the tundra, with wrists bound, from 5A.M. to 4 P.M. awaiting their unknown fate. I was one of them, now known as a priest who celebrated Mass openly.

Our punishment was to pound rock with sledgehammers twelve hours a day and sleep outdoors in the quarry itself. I was so exhausted I couldn't even eat. As this continued, I knew I was nearing a complete breakdown. I drifted away from the other prisoners while they ate and as I lay awake alone near nightfall I saw a small nest filled with chicks and then the papa bird flew in to feed them. This gentle care of these smallest creatures filled me with joy, and there in this wasteland I remembered my own father making me breakfast that morning I returned at 1A.M. after almost being killed in a train tunnel. I started crying remembering too all my fellow prisoners shot and others killed by their own hands. At that moment a fellow quarry workmate found me and slapped me on the shoulder, encouraging me to join the others to eat. I looked up as he carelessly picked up a rock and winged it at the bird's nest that had brought me such welcome joy. I exploded in rage at him for his wanton cruelty. I was so furious I could have strangled him, but he backed off and took off. I collapsed, frightened at my own rage.

My depression lasted for two more days, but when Sunday came with its day of rest I took a bath in a quarry pool followed by a long sleep in the sunlight. I slept like a baby and woke hours later more sane but still shaken. I barely shook off this breakdown. All I could pray was "Give us this day our daily bread." I ate that night for the first time in days.

Shortly after this episode, the quarry brigade returned to Camp #5. The crack down had worked, but so did the strikes and the new era post-Stalin conciliation began with granting many of the workers' demands. Pay for extra work and reduced sentences were doled out and work morale improved. A pay-as-you-earned store opened and with my first rubles in hand I bought a loaf of rye bread and ate it all at one sitting. A friend named Misha altered my health records of my blood pressure to ease my work load, and when this deception was detected I was relocated to Kayerkhan.

Kayerkhan meant working below ground in the coal mines. The beginning of my fifteen years of hard labor sentence had begun with shoveling coal into barges. Now that I was in the final year of my sentence,

I descended into those cellars where the coal was mined by blasting and pic ax. Our new brigade was schooled for a few weeks in mining methods and safety procedures and then we were lowered down the mine shafts in shaky cages to the labyrinth of dark tunnels where you had to crouch and crawl to the work zone. Nightmares were frequent and came true when a ceiling collapsed on me and I was nearly killed. How many times would God not let me die?

Days later I heard the timbers crack and a Chinese laborer feet from me was crushed. When we unburied him I saw that his spine had snapped and was protruding. So much for our classroom crash course in precautions.

Despite better conditions in the camp, I got scurvy complicated by all the stress and sleepless night sweats. I had somehow kept a small prayer book from my seminary days, always concealing it until a young guard caught me mumbling my night prayers. He snatched it from me.

I just couldn't bear to lose that last token of innocence. Looking up into his face all I said was "I am a priest." He tossed it back for me to keep. I thanked God for this mercy and nodded thanks to the guard.

There were three other priests and two Orthodox monks at Kayerkhan and we celebrated Mass almost daily. Knowing how back breaking and dangerous our labor was, restrictions were greatly eased in the camp and privileges for extra work increased. As Christmas approached we were informed by the grapevine that we could celebrate a Mass for the whole barrack to raise spirits of any who might want to attend. Many of the men, like myself, were near the end of their sentence and there literally was light at the end of the tunnel. Many attended the Midnight Christmas Mass and as they sang the ancient Russian hymns some little gleam of hope still squinted from their eyes in the candlelight. There is no hope like hope that lives with despair daily.

Several days later, so exhausted from working in the mines, I fell asleep riding the coal conveyor belt which we were forbidden to do. I was almost dumped down a shaft and weeks later there was a flash explosion that knocked me unconscious for close to two hours. How many more times would I escape death? Would this be my tomb before Resurrection? Before my release?

It was the Spring of 1955 and I was a fifty-one year old worn out wreck. Dr. Janos examined me after the explosion and told me that I had to get out of the mines or I wouldn't survive another three months. He put me on a sick list but an official insisted that I go back to work. Dr. Janos put in writing that this would be my death sentence and that that official would be investigated and reprimanded.

After Dr. Janos' threat to report the official if I died, I was transferred to my last labor in Siberia, not below the earth but in a stable. Never had I worked around horses and the other farm-boy prisoners laughed at my timidity especially around a Mongolian horse called Vashka. That horse had a crazy look and when I had to enter his stall to feed him he kicked so furiously I ran out. One old horse-hand took pity on me and told me to enter the stall shouting every obscenity I knew as loud as I could and to wave my arms more than Vasha kicked. I was afraid but did it screaming wildly the worst street slang from my teen years in Shenandoah. Poor Vasha met a creature more crazy than himself and backed off hugging the wall of the stable while I dropped the food pail and strutted out still cursing. The bluff worked.

The next day I was given official notice that because of my exceptional work record over the years my sentence had been reduced to fourteen years and nine months. Those last three months might have killed me but I was spared by God's Providence.

The night before I left, my mining comrades and my fellow priests gave me a going away party and then I celebrated my last prison Mass. Next morning, at 9 A.M. I was led to the exit station, given a small packet of letters and photos dated 1949 from my parish in Poland and a Restricted Passport Certificate. As a confessed and convicted spy I had served my sentence of hard labor, but I would never be free to leave Russia or come and go as I pleased.

As I left the prison compound of the camp I still walked like a prisoner with my hands clasped behind my back with head down looking not ahead but at the ground underfoot. I heard the guards in the tower laughing at me because I didn't know how to walk like a free man with head up and arms at my sides.

I walked to the train station, purchased a ticket with my rubles from hard labor of fourteen years and nine months, for the city of Norilsk. When the train began to move I expected it to jerk to a halt and a guard would appear to return me to prison. The only guard to appear was a woman ticket conductor who even smiled when she clipped my ticket. I sat very still, closed my eyes and wept. Without any beads, I prayed all fifteen decades of the Rosary my Polish mother had taught me before my seminary days and then I fell sound asleep as the train rumbled on.

CHAPTER EIGHT

A FREE MAN—RESTRICTED

My destination was the city of Norilsk at the foot of Mt. Schmidtika in the Arctic Circle. I had helped build that city's apartment houses when I was a prisoner. I remembered pouring the cement foundation of these apartments praying that it wouldn't freeze up too quickly and then crack. The smoke from all the new factories covered everything with dirty snow. Man's smudge was everywhere. As I walked the streets, still in my prison issued padded suit, I felt out of place, an alien. Finally I found Fr. Victor's *bolok*, a shack he shared with another priest, Fr. Neron. They had been released from prison two months prior to my release and had gotten word to me of their address. The *bolok* was 10' by 10' but had a roof, two beds, three wooden chairs, and a coal stove for cooking and heat. These priests welcomed me and we pushed the beds together as an altar and celebrated Mass, in peace, with no spies, just angels, I'm sure. We slept upright in those chairs but I felt at home. On Sunday we celebrated Mass for our make-shift parish of sixty members in a chapel these Poles had salvaged there among the *boloks*.

Next morning I reported to the police station as required by my Restricted Certificate. The MVD police informed me of further restrictions, namely statute 58:6 which stipulated that I was to live only where I was told. I was also warned against performing priestly activities.

I began making friends almost immediately. Our next store neighbor was Ludwig, the choirmaster, and his wife and two Lithuanian women who cared for an old Orthodox priest, Fr. Foma. I then quickly sought out five young Poles I had known in prison and they invited me to live with them in their spacious 10' x 12' *bolok* and I accepted. There were only two beds but you slept in the bed vacated by the on duty worker, in rotation. Always a warm bed, they joked. The advantage here was that we ate our meals in a nearby barrack and I didn't have to impose on my two priest friends.

I then met a young Pole named Ladislas who was working in the *B.O.F.* factory, another building that I had helped build during my prison days. He encouraged me to seek work in the laboratory and that was a Godsend.

The following Sunday I again celebrated Mass for our Polish parish and they wanted to give me rubles to support their priest but I refused. They then insisted on buying me decent clothes if I insisted on working besides being their priest. After celebrating the first of many memorial Requiem services for their dead, a beautiful sung liturgy I knew from my *Russicum* seminary days, I headed for the *B.O.F.* laboratory for a job interview.

The woman supervisor was named Anastasia and she was a total professional and also quite beautiful. After a brief description of my education and sundry prison occupations, especially my stint in the pharmacy and early release for an exceptional work record, she offered me a job filing chemical test results with a salary of $110 dollars per month. I didn't hesitate and we shook hands. She told me to report for work the next morning at the late hour of 8 A.M. No more iron gong going off at 5 A.M. That wage scale for one month was close to what I had earned in prison for an entire year.

There were only three men in my section of the laboratory and forty girls but it was not forced labor and seemed like an industrious convent where courtesy and diligent work was expected from all. My job was to keep the girls supplied with chemicals and to file test results.

Gradually I relaxed and very soon the word spread that I was a priest and one of the young women privately asked me to conduct a memorial service for her recently deceased husband. Shortly after I baptized her only son. The Faith was still alive there in Norilsk, undernourished but alive. God wanted me here; this was why I was sent to Russia.

Now that I was settled in, I asked at the police station if I could write a letter to my sister in the States. After a four hour wait to see the MVD Chief I was granted permission and even treated to the proper mailing envelope for outside the USSR. Even the MVD could be kind on occasion. This would be my first letter home in fifteen years and I wrote to my sister who was a nun, Sr. Evangeline. I kept it very short and simple: "Alive and well. Your brother Walter." I expected the KGB would read everything I sent.

I told a fellow worker named Petro of my first letter home and he insisted that we have a celebratory drink at his home. His wife baked pilmeni and out came two water glasses filled to the brim with vodka. You toast, clink glass and then in two gulps, down the entire glass and quickly hold a piece of rye bread under your nose to soften the sting. We toasted the letter, America, etc., etc., etc. I was toasted too. Those toasts knocked me flat. Once was enough. No more rounds of toasts for me after that. Petro made sure I had a safe sleep.

Soon after, Ladislas was married and many of the working girls attended. More and more of them talked with me about Faith. To many of them Faith was an exotic relic, a forbidden topic, ridiculed in their schooling but remembered by their grandparents with reverence. I sensed that the grace of God was at work by my presence among them and in their seeking.

After a few months at the Laboratory I received an award *Blagodaros*, (Excellent Worker) and was invited to join the Union of Soviet Workers. With little hesitation I accepted. Norilsk had given me a steady job and even better, I now had my own parish to serve as a priest. I was invited to move in with the newlyweds for they had an entire spare room I could call my own. Since my cell in Lubianka I hadn't had a solitary space for prayer and this small room was my prayer sanctuary, especially on Sundays after the Parish Masses.

Soon after peace descended, the KGB questioned me concerning my missionary work, as they called it. I was surprised at how directly I confronted them with their own Constitution which guaranteed freedom of religion and freedom of conscience. They quickly countered that proselytizing was forbidden by that same Constitution and bluntly told me to drop all subversive activities. Had my open conversations with the laboratory staff been reported, I wondered? In quick succession, Fr. Victor and Fr. Neron were also interrogated. Had the growth of our little parish also been duly noted by the KGB? Of course! My own priestly work had doubled recently and I had even taken days off from laboratory work to catch up on priestly duties of Baptisms, Requiems, and Confessions. Being a new member of the Workers Union further exposed me to scrutiny. But this reprimand did not diminish my joy of finally being a shepherd for my flock. This was my calling.

A letter from the USA finally arrived. My sister, Sr. Evengeline, wrote that our family and the Jesuits had presumed that I was dead and now, like Lazarus, I had been returned to them. She asked if I needed anything at all. My letter had gotten across the ocean and passed KGB inspection. I was aware of my sister's careful circumspection and thanked God that we were, at long last, in touch.

No sooner had I replied to my sister asking for clothing than a big funeral for one of the Lithuanian leaders who had policed our *boloks* was requested by our parish. Suddenly we had a two hundred-voice men's choir singing the ancient liturgy and the KGB didn't bother to conceal their presence. Shortly after this public liturgy, Fr. Victor and Fr. Nerone would leave for the Ukraine. The KGB knew how to play chess and owned the board and all the players.

Since there were now more pastoral duties for me as the only priest, I moved into a small room close to the chapel but continued meals with Ladislas and his wife. Now the parishioners grew bolder and proposed to build an Orthodox church. To counter this boldness the KGB invited me to write articles about this project and the parish expansion. It was not difficult to see this entrapment giving the KGB grounds that I was proselytizing. I refused to cooperate with the KGB.

I continued my priestly ministry even when it meant baptizing at 2 A.M. after trudging through a snowstorm because I knew the entire family were there waiting for me, depending on their priest. They had been without far too long. I made it back for the 6 A.M. Mass in the chapel.

My sister, Sr. Evangeline, sent clothing and informed me that they, she and my sister Helen, had contacted the U.S. State Department and the American Embassy in Moscow to get me out. I was convinced that I was destined to spend my life tending my flock here in Russia but I began the process of seeking an International Passport and was told, "You're not going back. You will never get out." Convicted spies don't go home again.

That Lent of 1958 was my busiest ministry as a priest and the Easter Liturgy was a glorious explosion of hundreds of voices that swept me up in a joy I had never before experienced. The crowd was so great and the chapel so full I could hardly lift my arms to raise the Host at the Consecration. That Midnight Liturgy only concluded at 3 AM with all greeting each other with "*Kristos voskes*" (Indeed He is Risen) over and over into the dawn. I had been up for forty-eight hours straight with Confessions and preparations for this liturgy but I was never so happy in all my life as a priest. "*Kristos voskes*." I was beginning to live my dream of serving his flock in Russia. That was the dream begun when I first heard the call from Father General's letter back in my novitiate days at Wernersville, almost thirty years ago.

Days later while at work in the laboratory I was summoned. The KGB wants to see you now. A handsome KGB officer informed me: "You are to leave Norilsk in ten days. Quit your job immediately. You are to go to Krasnoyarsk." There was no discussion.

I said Mass every day until I left ten days later with a plane ticket courtesy of the KGB.

CHAPTER NINE

EXILED TO KRASNOYARSK

But before I left Norilsk I stopped to check on my mail. There were two envelopes, one addressed to Ciszek and the other to my assumed name of Lypinski, from the American Embassy in Moscow. They urged that I come to the Embassy in Moscow to pursue an exit visa. The KGB wanted me out of Norilsk immediately, so I boarded the plane for Krasnoyarsk.

This was my first flight ever and I was spellbound by the vast tundra of the severe Arctic North as we flew south to Krasnoyarsk. Twelve years ago I had made this same trip traveling from the south to the north in the hold of the ship *Stalin*. That sickening trip had taken over two weeks. This plane trip took just four hours to land at a modern brick and glass airport.

As I disembarked I felt my first warm softness of spring, and as I carried my two suitcases, one with my precious Mass kit and vestments, I began to perspire. Taxied to Hotel Syever. Booked a shared room for $1.50 and paid another $1.50 for a beef stroganov dinner and then sent a letter to my sisters and another to the American Embassy in Moscow telling them of my re-assignment to Krasnoyarsk after my sudden exit from Norilsk. Back at the hotel I met my roommate who said he was a business man; I wasn't so sure. We watched TV, had a beer at the bar and then retired.

The next morning I went to the Office of Foreign Visas at 8 A.M. and started filling out the required paperwork which took close to two hours. A nosy old man kept pestering me with questions prompted by his unabashed snooping of my documents. I finally bluntly stopped him cold by admitting that I was a priest who had been imprisoned. To my surprise he was delighted because he was a Lithuanian Catholic. He insisted that

I visit his home and rushed on telling me that their priest, Fr. Janos, had recently died.

A kind woman who received my documents at the Foreign Visa Office sadly told me: "You'll never see America again." And then, even more sadly added: "There is no life for you here in Russia." But she was wrong on both accounts. I would wait three months before hearing from the Foreign Visa office. The reply was starkly simple: "No. Request denied for Visa."

I returned to the hotel after promising to visit my new old Lithuanian friend. At the hotel I walked into the garden and sat still in the sunshine remembering that same warmth that day at the quarry where I had been saved from despair by the sight of the chicks being fed in their nest. Now I watched children playing with hoops skipping around a small fountain. Where to now? I asked God. I sat there a long time with no hint of an answer and once again remembered to surrender to his Providence that had rescued me so many times before. Thy will be done.

I decided to purchase a ticket to visit the American Embassy in Moscow and did so that afternoon. The next morning there was a message from the MVD to report to the police station. I was informed to cancel my ticket for Moscow; no explanation given. I had a Restricted Certificate of release from prison. They could jerk me around like a puppet on a string. I was ordered to stay put in Krasnoytarsk.

I visited the Catholic Lithuanian and he gathered others to greet me for dinner and they all insisted that I be their priest tending their parish in the village of Nikolayevka. Their parish had close to two hundred members and arrangements were made for me to live with a parishioner named Rosa. They showered me with food for a month and I gratefully celebrated Latin High Mass and Benedictions for them. God still wanted me there serving his remnant faithful. I continued priestly ministry and the numbers swelled to eight hundred at Masses.

A few month's later at 1 A.M. Rosa's guard dog barked in the night and a slightly drunk MVD officer rapped on the window to avoid the fierce dog at the gate. I let him in. Perhaps he hoped that I was in the wrong bedroom, but that was clearly not the case; he smirked and told me to be in his office at 3 P.M. that day at the Passport Bureau.

I did what I was told. His message: "You shouldn't have registered to live here in this village and your passport has been cancelled to stay here. You have forty-eight hours to get out of Krasnoyarsk." He mentioned nothing about the parish growth but that was the real offense: my priestly ministry.

As I walked back to Rosa's, dragging my feet with hands clasped behind my back and head down I felt like a prisoner all over again. I mumbled to myself: "When is this going to end?" They were clearly hounding me to death as long as I persisted in being a priest. This time they had given a choice of destination: Yeniseisk or Abakan. I choose Abakan because it was further South and warmer.

My parishioners saw me to the train station. I tried not to weep but their crying, their losing of another priest, broke my heart. God help them. God help me help them. The power of evil was driving me away; the KGB was its tool. Once again, en route praying for the faithful remnant of Krasnoyarsk. God was in their heart and he was why they had stayed so faithful.

Once again, I fell asleep to the rhythm of train wheels.

CHAPTER TEN

REPRIEVE IN ABAKAN

The train ride from Krasnoyarsk to Abakan took twelve restless hours. The KGB were relentlessly shutting every door that opened to my serving as a priest. I looked out the train windows as we sped by the Sayan Mountains heading further South. We arrived at 6 P.M. in Abakan which is just North of Mongolia. The faces of the native people at the station clearly looked Mongolian with narrow eyes, broad cheekbones and sun-dried skin. I waited an hour for a taxi to get to the one hotel. I could have walked; the ride took all of five minutes but I hadn't asked anyone so I got taken. I was clearly an outsider and the hotel manager told me, without apology, that no room was available. Did I look that suspicious? Was the KGB closing even this door? I was feeling paranoid, nonetheless.

I walked the streets looking for a friendly face but found none. I spotted the MVD headquarters around 11 P.M. and inquired about lodging. They checked my Restricted Certificate and turned me out warning me to beware of thieves and dogs on the streets at night, cynically adding "Good Luck" as I walked out to those streets. I felt helpless and psychologically abandoned. Sitting on a bench I prayed, my head in my hands with my two bags squeezed tight between my feet for safe-keeping. I prayed to the only Friend I knew I had in Abakan.

As midnight approached, I asked a passerby who hadn't avoided me if he might take me in for the night. Stepan was the name of this Khakassian good Samaritan. His wife was very wary and reluctant, but they took me in and next day Stepan assured me that I could stay until I found a permanent room. I didn't tell them I was a priest and I later found out that the wife had thought I must be a thief hiding out in Abakan because I was so *captivo*.

Days later I followed up on a posted notice for lodging with a couple, Iosip and his wife Valya and sister Maria. The price was steep, $10. per month and $5 for meals per month. I'm serious, that was steep, but I had my own small room so I took it on the spot. It took a month for us to become friends but I still didn't tell them I was a priest and only celebrated Mass nightly after they were all asleep.

I had saved my salary from the laboratory in Norilsk and decided to take a year's vacation from all work. The KGB had forbidden me to do any priestly work and I was bone tired. Tired in body and in soul too. I felt old, old beyond my fifty-four years. All that work in coal mines and work crews outside in forty degrees below zero had taken its toll. My knees were giving out, so I spent time sitting in the warm sunlight, reading, and stretching these tired limbs.

Iosip was very active in local politics and semi-retired so there were many visitors at the house. We shared meals and I enjoyed all the company. With his introduction and at his table I made many friends and the conversations were lively about the new regime in Moscow with all the changes and the local intrigues, which I steered clear of.

By the Spring of 1959 I felt rested and was ready to look for a job but first decided to revisit my old parish and friends in Krasnoyarsk for just three days. I soon realized on that trip that the militia from MVD was tracking my every move and reporting to the KGB. In Krasnoyarsk when I looked up an old priest friend I found the KGB in his apartment. They did not explain where he was and took me to headquarters for questioning until 3 A.M. with further warnings about priestly subversive activity. I took the earliest train back to Abakan feeling my paranoia was completely justified.

One of Iosip's visitors worked at the large City Garage and suggested that I seek work there. The KGB preferred productive comrades not idle priests. The supervisor at the Garage, a big handsome and outgoing man named Petruchin took one look at my worker's rough hands and healthy look and took me on. I learned on the job as a mechanic with lots of coaching by comrades, some of whom had been prisoners too. I still kept my sentence as a Vatican Spy to myself and told no one that I was a priest. So I was set, for a while, at the City Garage, ATK-50. Little did I know then that this was to be my last job in Russia.

That was the Summer of 1959, and then another letter from my sister Helen arrived proposing that she planned to visit Moscow very soon. I couldn't sleep that night I was so excited at the prospect of her visit. It had been over twenty years since I had seen any of my family. The final torturous intrigue was just beginning.

CHAPTER ELEVEN

ABAKAN—1960 TO 1963 EXIT

Late in 1959 a letter from the American Embassy in Moscow arrived informing me that they had reached an agreement with the Soviet Foreign Office for my release to go to the USA if requested. I wrote to the Foreign Office asking them to grant me a Visa for a return visit to the USA. The run-around began: the Foreign Office sent my request to the Office of the Interior (KGB). Heard nothing from KGB for three months until I was summoned to MVD headquarters: the reply was negative with no explanation. During that three-month wait I made my semi-annual visit to the Passport Bureau to renew my short term passport. Out of the blue they suggested I get a permanent passport which I declined since that would further entrench me as a willing Soviet citizen. Beware favors from bureaucrats! Round and round the letters went and I went on with my work at the garage.

Since quotas were not being met at the garage there was a massive reshuffling and public, humiliating firings. Even the boss who hired me, Petruchin, was fired but I put my head down and worked my tail off, as usual, and even got an award for outstanding service translated as Shock Troop of Communist Labor Award. My name was added to the framed list in the Worker's Hall and my comrades mocked me with salutes. But one of my worker friends warned me: "Don't let them catch you listening to the Voice of America." Everybody seemed to know that I was being watched by the KGB. Even my lodging owner, Iosip, began suggesting that I find other housing because as a Party Member he was under scrutiny for housing a convicted spy. Fortunately I found a private room next store with Dmitri and his wife Illyena and his old *babushka*, his mother, who mothered me with her never-ending bowls of hot soup: potatoes, cabbage, beets, onions, and lamb bones covered in lard. Here too I had privacy for prayer and nightly Mass and on Sundays I read the Bible to my heart's content without interruption. But everywhere else I was being watched by the MVD and KGB. Was a priest really that much of a threat or were they looking for an excuse to validate blocking my visa requests?

A bright spot came at work one afternoon when I met a Professor, a Polish expatriate, who was an archeologist at the Abakan Museum. He had dropped in at the garage because he needed a key made for a display case at the museum, hoping that some craftsman might oblige. We became close friends and I stamped a key for him and later procured from the States research books from Jesuits in Washington, D.C. He called himself an atheist and pressed me to marry a lady friend, who was forty-five, who would care for me in my impending old age. I laughed it off and he gave up for the time being. At times we argued about religion but he later told me that I was the one really true friend he had ever made. I enjoyed our many conversations and debates. Our Polish genes kicked in, I suppose.

Then in April of 1963, a letter from my sister Helen arrived telling me that she had received a visa to visit Russia and would be in Moscow on June 19 and asked me to meet her there. I was so excited at the prospect of meeting one of my own family that I hadn't seen in over twenty years. Would I ever get permission for this visit to Moscow, and would my supervisor at work allow me time off since I already had used up my allotted vacation time? I even contemplated just quitting my job if I had to. I couldn't bear to think that I might miss Helen when she was so close. I pressed my superior at the garage and after a month of delaying he and a committee made me an exception because of my outstanding work status and granted me a twelve-day leave. They were nervous that I might slip up, and bad press might embarrass them with the KGB. I assured them that I could be trusted, and my word was respected by them.

That night I offered Mass and deliberately didn't pray that I would see my sister Helen. After all the lessons learned at Lubianka and the Siberian camps, I finally trusted God's Providence. I no longer tried to bend His will to my own. Surrender to his will was now my only desire. I trusted him with every detail of my life. Surrender was now deeply encoded in my bones.

I heard nothing from Helen and still bought a train ticket to Moscow for Sunday, June 16, and that very morning as I left my courtyard for the station, a girl approached asking: "Does Walter Ciszek live here?" She had a telegram from Washington, D.C. which I tore open to find that the only message was all in numbers. Was this a KGB joke? I raced to the local post office and what seemed like hours later the telegram was decoded: "Encountering delays. Will keep you informed. Helen." I stayed put.

Another letter didn't arrive until a month later and it was from my other sister, Sister Evangeline. She was coming with Helen, but because of delays with her visa they had to postpone the trip. She promised to let me know when they would be coming. She promised that they would be coming. Who was pulling the strings? My solution: God!

That night, when I told my friends Iosip and Dmitri, that both of my sisters would be visiting me in Moscow soon, Iosip said: "They must be going to try and get you out," and Dmitri retorted, "No chance." He then added, "Perhaps, sometime later, if our government has to make an exchange for one of our own men, they might possibly give you up." Thus, a prophet spoke in Abakan. To me, returning permanently to America was not a reality. Seeing my sisters in Moscow was reality enough to hope for.

June, July, and August passed quickly, and then on a September afternoon at work, at 3 P.M. another worker approached me and said ominously, "Tovarisch wants to see you now, right away." Tovarisch exited his own office as I arrived, and there was a KGB official at his desk. Without any preliminaries he informed me that the KGB General wanted to see me at 4 P.M. at the hotel in Abakan, that afternoon.

The General greeted me, "Vladimir Martinovich come right in." Another KGB officer, Viktor Pavlovich began: "We would like to do you a favor and grant you an exit visa." He smilingly explained how things were different now from the rigid Stalin by-gone days. I simply stated that I had lived in Russia for twenty-three years and never complained. They looked at each other and the General excused himself. Pavlovich wanted to see me again at the hotel at 4:30 P.M. the next day.

At the second meeting Pavlovich, still smiling, began with the words, "Of course, we expect you to return the favor." My skin crawled. I didn't even reply. He continued, "Go to Moscow, go to Confession if you like. You should loosen up and have a wonderful time. Visit all the priests you like. We have their addresses for you." "All you have to do is report your impressions of them to us on your return." I sat still as a statue looking directly in his eyes. He noticed that I was angry but simply suggested that I think it over until we met again. I left depressed and furious that the KGB were still trying to use me in such a blatant blackmail scheme in exchange for a visit with my sisters and promise of an exit visa. I only found out later that my sisters had already been in Moscow and had even seen Premier Krushchev.

That night I had the worst nightmare of my life in which Viktor Pavlovich was smilingly exposing disgusting scandals of Moscow priests that I had delivered to the KGB. When I woke, I resolved to tell the KGB that I didn't want their favors and that I was sick of the whole business.

Another KGB official, Aleksandr Mihailovich, interrogated me soon after, assuring me of their innocent intentions and I flatly told him, "I don't believe a word you say." After this three-hour interview I stood up and said: "Words won't convince me. No deal." I walked out without his permission. No more meetings followed, and during the rest of September and October I resolved to stop wishful thinking. They opened the door to a visit with my sisters and even an exit visa and I had shut that door myself. "*Finito*" I thought.

I was in my apartment room reading at 9:30 P.M. when I was startled by a rapping at the window next to where I was reading and saw a KGB officer peering in. I opened the side door and he addressed me, "Vladimir Martinovich, I've come to get you. Get in the car." I obviously had no choice in the matter. Was this my "*finito*"? We drove in silence back to the hotel and Alexsandr Mihailovich met me.

There was no more discussion of favors or deals. He bluntly told me "Quit your job at ATK-50 tomorrow. Pay your debts. Buy a plane ticket for Krasnoyarsk. I'll meet you at the airport. You are going to Moscow." That was it. No mention of my sisters, nothing further about a visa. He snapped his fingers and his aide brought in cognac, cake, and chocolates to seal the bargain. After one sip of cognac I put my hand over my glass: no more for me. I had been drugged before with tea and cookies in Lubianka. Mihailovich, unsmiling, nodded to his aide and the aide ushered me out into a KGB car. Was I going to be shot and then just disappear? I bowed my head and surrendered, not to the KGB but to God's Providence. That was Thursday night. In silence, I was delivered back to my apartment.

Sunday, Dimitri and family, my beloved *babuska* who had fed me all those hot soups, and Iosip and his wife, my Professor friend, and several fellow workers from the garage, gave me a send-off party. Poor *babuska* cried and drank, drank and cried, and then we had to ease her to bed. She wasn't the only one crying. When all left, I retired to my room, rested a bit and then rose to celebrate a Mass of Thanksgiving for these beloved Russian friends.

The Professor wouldn't let me leave alone on the bus to the airport and once there he embraced me in full view of the KGB. I boarded at 11 A.M. for Kayerkhan for the fifty-five minute flight and there was met at the airport by Aleksandr who handed me a plane ticket for Moscow leaving tomorrow. He said I was free to visit old friends there in Kayerkhan, and I gladly did so stopping at my old parish and was welcomed by Rosa and many parishioners. By 11 P.M. I was back in the hotel, wrote postcards to friends in Abakan, entrusted tomorrow to God and slept soundly.

Aleksandr saw me off at my 7 A.M. flight for Moscow and as we lifted off my spirits lightened. Hadn't God's Providence safe-guarded me all these twenty-three years in Russia where He had called me to be a priest? I started praying the Rosary, but a deluxe meal was served and this borscht, covered with lard eater of yesterday, tasted chicken Kiev, blintz and caviar.

At Vnukova Airport in Moscow, I disembarked and saw no one I knew and then Viktor Pavlovich stepped up and greeted me. Kuznetsov, another KGB official was beside him. They were quite pleasant on the twenty-five mile drive from the airport to Moscow and acted like tourist guides pointing out the vast Lenin University campus. We reached the Moscow Hotel in under two hours. They told me to be back at the hotel at 5 P.M. so I had time to shower and then strolled about looking for something to eat. At 5 P.M. Kuznetsov returned and we attended a performance of *Mary Stuart* at the Moscow Dramatic Theatre. Nothing was said of why I was being wined and dined, and I knew better than to ask.

The next day, on my own, I was free to be a tourist. I had spent five years in Moscow but that had been inside Lubianka prison. Now, those bells I had heard tolling then could be seen and heard tolling from the Kremlin. I visited the old Orthodox onion-domed churches. It was sad to see how God had been removed from his own house by the USSR. But had he? I knew God would never desert Holy Mother Russia as I prayed there in these still-sacred places.

Two days later, after more sightseeing, concerts and dinners, Kuznetsov told me that tomorrow he had something to tell me. He then added, "Get rid of all your money except ninety rubles." I didn't ask why. I visited Lenin's tomb, the Father of the Revolution, and I prayed for him thinking, "He was a man, after all, and maybe in need of more prayers than he's getting." I then went to GUM, the renowned department store and attempted to spend my hard-earned-and-saved four hundred rubles. It took me four times around that vast store to spend my rubles on an overcoat, shoes, a watch, a camera, razor blades, a valise, and even a fedora.

At 9 A.M. on October 3, Kusnetsov met me at my hotel room and took all my documents, including my Worker's Award certificate and verified I had spent all my rubles. I had only three left. We departed for the Mezdunarodni Airport which I knew had international flights. As we approached the airport, Kusnetsov leaned over and said quietly, "if you want to stay . . . you might have a hard time there." Was I going home? I dismissed the thought. Then he said, "If you go, you can come back."

We stepped out of the car. It was 4 P.M. and a well-suited gentleman, non-Russian, stepped forward and greeted me. "Father Ciszek. I'm glad to meet you. I'm Mr. Kirk from the American Consulate in Moscow. We have some papers for you to sign." Inside, another American diplomat, Marvin McKinem, also greeted me as "Father Ciszek." I began signing the papers, not even reading them just as I had not read the hundred-page "Confession" I had signed back in Lubianka. Now I knew who to trust. The signing completed, Mr. Kirk shook my hand again and said, "You're an American citizen." It was like a fairy-tale. I felt as if I ought to sing. Instead, I waved my last three rubles and invited all, American diplomats and KGB officials, to tea, on me.

Almost all were talking and smiling. Was I dreaming this?

A huge BOAC jetlliner slowly slid into place and Mr. McKinem and I boarded, First Class! I buckled up and we fell silent as the plane lifted off, and as it banked I saw the spires of the Kremlin. I made the Sign of the Cross, not on myself, but over the land I loved and was leaving forever. It was October 3, 1963. I started saying the Rosary, but wept silently and then fell into a deep sleep, lulled by the jet engines' powerful humming.

I later learned that as my plane flew west, another jet flew east with two Russian spies freed by the U.S. Government in exchange for this priest. Dmitri's prophecy had come true.

I lived to tell my story with the help of my fellow Jesuit, Father Daniel Flaherty, and published *With God in Russia* and *He Leadeth Me.*

Father Walter Ciszek lived safe, secure, and happy as a Jesuit priest in the United States of America until his eightieth year when God called him home on December 8, 1984, Feast of the Immaculate Conception. Set free at last, his remains rest at the Novitiate, St. Isaac Jogues, Wernersville, Pennsylvania where he first heard God calling him to Russia.

Father Walter Ciszek, S.J. - A free man, U.S.A. 1963.

APPENDIX

SIGNIFICANT EVENTS
IN WALTER CISZEK'S LIFE

Born on November 4, 1904. Shenandoah, Pa.

Entered Jesuits on September 7, 1928. St. Andrew on Hudson, Poughkeepsie, N.Y.

At Wernersville, Pa., during his second year of Novitiate, hears letter of Jesuit General, Father Wlodimir Ledochowski inviting future priests to volunteer to enter Communist U.S.S.R. 1930.

Takes Vows in Society of Jesus at St. Isaac Jogues Novitiate, Wernersville, Pa. 1930.

Theological studies at the Gregorian University and Russian studies at Russicum, Rome, Italy. 1934.

Ordained in Rome, June 23, 1937. Volunteers to enter Poland as a priest.

American Embassy warns all Americans to leave Poland with immanent arrival of Germans and Russians. 1938.

Enters Russia on March 19, 1940, Feast of St. Joseph.

Arrested by K.G.B. as suspected spy and jailed at Chusovoy. 1941.

Intered in Moscow's Lubianka Prison. 1941.

Signs Confession at Lubianka, July 26, 1942.

Detained at Lubianka. Refuses to be a counter-spy. Sentenced to fifteen years at hard labor in Siberia, 1946. Transported to Siberian prison camps in Arctic Circle.

Presumed dead by Jesuits in U.S.A. 1947.

Soviet Premier, Joseph Stalin dies. March, 1953.

Released from prison after fourteen years and nine months, April 22, 1955.

As a convicted spy, must remain in Russia with a Restricted Passport. Ordered to Norilsk, still in the Arctic. 1955.

Sends first letter home to Jesuits and sisters in U.S.A. 1955.

K.G.B. warns Walter Ciszek to stop priestly activities, 1957.

Lent/Easter, 1958, "busiest as a priest." A Glorious Easter.

American Embassy informs Walter Ciszek to obtain an Exit visa. April, 1958.

Sister proposes a visit to Russia, July, 1959.

American Embassy informs Walter Ciszek that there is an 'agreement for release if requested'. Summer, 1959.

Walter Ciszek exits Russia on October 3, 1963.

Arrives in America on October 12, 1963.

Publishes, with co-author Father Daniel Flaherty, S.J., *With God in Russia*, The American Press, 1964.

Publishes, with co-author Father Daniel Flaherty, S.J., *He Leadeth Me*, Doubleday & Company, 1973.

Walter Ciszek enters eternity on Dec. 8, Feast of the Immaculate Cenception, 1984. His eighty year journey completed.

CPSIA information can be obtained
at www.ICGtesting.com
Printed in the USA
LVHW032331100623
749444LV00005B/215